Original title:
The Joy of Being

Copyright © 2024 Creative Arts Management OÜ
All rights reserved.

Author: Helena Marchant
ISBN HARDBACK: 978-9916-88-986-2
ISBN PAPERBACK: 978-9916-88-987-9

Canvas of Possibilities

On a canvas bare and wide,
Dreams and wishes collide.
Colors swirl, vibrant and bold,
Stories waiting to be told.

Brushes dance in hands so free,
Painting hopes for all to see.
Each stroke a chance, a new embrace,
Transforming fears, erasing space.

Whispers of futures yet unseen,
In every hue, a chance to glean.
From shadows deep to shining light,
Creating paths that feel just right.

As we paint this grand design,
Life unfolds, a thread divine.
With every layer, we explore,
A canvas rich with endless lore.

Tides of Thankfulness

With every wave, a gift we'll find,
Gratitude flows, gentle and kind.
The sun sinks low, painting the sky,
In this moment, hearts learn to fly.

Whispers of joy dance on the shore,
Nature's embrace, forever more.
Each breath we take, a sweet refrain,
In tides of thankfulness, we remain.

Seasons of Delight

Spring brings blooms, a vibrant show,
Summer's warmth, where laughter flows.
Autumn leaves in hues so bold,
Winter's chill, a tale retold.

Each season paints our canvas bright,
Echoes of joy, pure delight.
Through time's embrace, we find our way,
In every moment, dance and play.

Breathing Life into Laughter

Laughter bubbles, bright and free,
A melody of joy, a symphony.
With every chuckle, hearts unite,
In moments shared, we find our light.

A playful wink, a silly face,
Brings warmth and love, a sweet embrace.
In laughter's glow, our spirits soar,
Breathing life, forever more.

Dreaming with Open Eyes

In daylight's glow, dreams take flight,
With open eyes, we chase the light.
Visions dance like shadows cast,
Moments cherished, forever last.

With every heartbeat, dreams align,
Stories woven, yours and mine.
Together we weave a tapestry,
In dreaming bright, we wander free.

The Light Within

In the silence of the dawn,
A flicker starts to glow,
Within the heart it lingers,
A warmth only we know.

Through shadows cast by doubt,
The light begins to rise,
Illuminating paths ahead,
Reflecting in our eyes.

With every step we take,
The brilliance shines anew,
Unveiling all our dreams,
In hues of gold and blue.

Embrace the light inside,
Let it guide your way,
For in the depths of you,
Is where the truth will stay.

Grains of Time

Each moment slips away,
Like sand through fingers fine,
A treasure not to waste,
Cherished like aged wine.

In laughter and in tears,
The grains of life will blend,
Together we will weave,
The stories that won't end.

With every ticking clock,
We shape our precious fate,
In quiet whispers shared,
We learn to love, not hate.

So hold the present close,
Embrace the fleeting hour,
For in these grains of time,
We find our truest power.

Tapestry of Contentment

In colors soft and bright,
We weave our daily dreams,
With threads of joy and hope,
Life flows in quiet streams.

Each stitch a gentle peace,
A moment deeply felt,
In simple acts of love,
The warmth of hearts will melt.

Through trials that we face,
We find our strength to grow,
In every shade and hue,
True beauty starts to show.

A tapestry unfolds,
With stories every day,
In contentment, we find joy,
And let our worries sway.

Waves of Serenity

In the stillness of the sea,
Soft waves begin to play,
Whispers of the ocean breeze,
Guide our minds away.

With every gentle rise,
A moment's breath is found,
The rhythm of the water,
A peaceful, soothing sound.

Underneath the vast blue sky,
We learn to simply be,
As time drifts like a tide,
We flow effortlessly.

So let your worries wash,
Upon the sandy shore,
In the waves of serenity,
Find solace evermore.

Flourishing in Stillness

In quietude, the heart finds peace,
Amidst the whispers, joys increase.
A gentle breeze, the mind's retreat,
In stillness, life feels pure and sweet.

Beneath the surface, flowers bloom,
In silent corners, dreams consume.
A tranquil space for thoughts to spin,
Where time dissolves, and calm begins.

Unraveling the Paradoxes

In shadows bright, the truth unfolds,
With every story, mystery holds.
Joy in sorrow, light in dark,
Life's tender dance leaves a mark.

Conflicted minds, yet hearts entwined,
In chaos, patterns undefined.
The stillness found in fray and fuss,
In paradox, we learn to trust.

Kaleidoscope of Feelings

Colors swirl in vivid dream,
Ephemeral moments, like a stream.
Joy and sorrow, woven tight,
In every change, a thrilling sight.

Flashes of laughter, echoes of pain,
A symphony played in the rain.
Each emotion, a vibrant hue,
In life's canvas, ever new.

Heartbeats of Happiness

In every pulse, a joy emerges,
With every heartbeat, life converges.
Laughter dances in the air,
In simple moments, love laid bare.

A sunshine smile, a warm embrace,
In every corner, we find grace.
Echoes of joy, a sweet refrain,
In heartbeats' rhythm, we remain.

Flickering Candles

In the dark, they flicker bright,
Whispers dance in dimmed light,
Shadows cast on walls of stone,
Each flame a story, softly known.

Hope ignites within their glow,
Guiding hearts where love may flow,
Moments captured, time stands still,
A gentle warmth, a perfect thrill.

Facing storms, they bend but stand,
Flickering like an artist's hand,
Crafting dreams in hues of gold,
Tales of warmth, forever told.

As night deepens, they play their part,
Lighting the corners of the heart,
In their dance, we find our peace,
Flickering candles that never cease.

Embrace of the Present

In the now, we breathe in deep,
Moments fleeting, ours to keep,
Time a river, flowing fast,
In the present, joy is cast.

Gentle whispers in the breeze,
Nature's song puts the soul at ease,
Grateful hearts for simple things,
In each moment, love it brings.

Let the past fade into wait,
Tomorrow shines, but don't be late,
Embrace this hour, feel its grace,
In the now, we find our place.

Together here, we laugh and share,
In this space, we feel the air,
Life unfolds in vibrant hues,
The present's gift, ours to choose.

Constellations of Purpose

Stars above, they twinkle bright,
Mapping dreams in the velvet night,
Each point a wish, a calling grand,
Constellations drawn by fate's hand.

Guiding sailors, lost at sea,
In their glow, we learn to be,
Navigating through the flow,
Finding paths that help us grow.

Every heartbeat tells a tale,
In the cosmos, we set sail,
Connected souls in vast array,
Chasing light, we find our way.

In the dark, our purpose gleams,
Fueling passion, igniting dreams,
Together we will rise and shine,
Constellations, your star and mine.

The Pulse of Stillness

In quiet times, we find our breath,
A subtle dance, embracing depth,
In stillness, thoughts begin to flow,
The pulse of life, a gentle glow.

Nature whispers, secrets shared,
In the calm, we feel prepared,
Moments stretch, like silk unfold,
In silence, truths of life are told.

Time slows down, the heart beats strong,
In the hush, we hear the song,
Harmony in every sigh,
The pulse of stillness lifts us high.

As the world spins, we stand apart,
Finding peace within the heart,
In stillness, we begin to see,
The pulse of life, our destiny.

Vibrant Echoes of Life

Whispers dance in the breeze,
Colors burst on the scene,
Heartbeat of the wild trees,
Nature's vibrant routine.

Moments flash like a spark,
Laughter fills the bright air,
Joy ignites the silent dark,
Life's rhythm, a sweet affair.

Eyes twinkle with delight,
Stories woven in the sky,
Each day brings fresh insight,
Underneath the sun's sly eye.

Embrace the noise around,
Let it stir your weary heart,
In this vivid world abound,
Life's echoes, a work of art.

Sunshine Through the Soul

Morning light spills like gold,
Gentle warmth upon the skin,
A tender touch, bright and bold,
Whispers of where love has been.

Clouds drift softly away,
Casting shadows on the past,
Hope rises with each new day,
A beacon that will ever last.

Life's canvas, brushed with grace,
Colors vivid, pure and bright,
Sunshine glows on each face,
Illuminating the night.

Through the windows of the heart,
Golden rays of dreams unfold,
With each moment, a fresh start,
Sunshine's gift, worth more than gold.

Journey into Bliss

Step by step, we ascend,
Paths uncharted, brave and wide,
With the heart as our friend,
We find joy on this ride.

Mountains high, valleys low,
Every twist a chance to see,
In the rhythm, we will flow,
Embracing what will be.

Waves of laughter, tears in tow,
Memories echo through the air,
In each moment, love will grow,
A tapestry rich and rare.

Navigating through the night,
Stars above, our guiding light,
With each challenge, we take flight,
Journey's end feels just so right.

Canvas of Today

Brushes dipped in vibrant hues,
Every stroke tells a story,
Unfolding dreams, endless views,
In the light of fleeting glory.

Moments captured, lost in time,
Here we are, alive and free,
Colors blend in perfect rhyme,
Life's canvas, a legacy.

Shadows linger, soften bright,
Shapes and forms begin to shine,
In the chaos, find the light,
A masterpiece, yours and mine.

Each dawn brings a new design,
Crafting dreams with every breath,
In this space, our souls align,
Creating life that conquers death.

Melodies in Movement

Notes like water flow, soft and light,
Carrying whispers through the night.
Every step a story told,
In rhythms warm, and moments bold.

Echoes dance upon the breeze,
Fluttering leaves in joyful tease.
Hearts entwined in gentle sway,
Lost together, come what may.

Chasing dreams in twilight's glow,
With every breath, let music grow.
In unison, we find our way,
Melodies guide us, come what may.

Embracing the Unpredictable

Life's wild tide, a shifting course,
Brings surprises, a hidden force.
With open arms, we greet the change,
Finding beauty in the strange.

Moments twist and turn like streams,
In woven paths of untold dreams.
Fear gives way to hopeful light,
As shadows dance into the night.

Each turn a chance, each fall a rise,
Beneath the stormy, swirling skies.
Embrace the chaos, hold it dear,
In every heartbeat, love draws near.

Shimmering Moments of Now

Glistening stardust fills the air,
As time spins softly, unaware.
In a glance, the world ignites,
Shimmering dreams on starry nights.

Every heartbeat, a fleeting trace,
Capturing life's delicate grace.
In now's embrace, we find our peace,
A tapestry that never ceases.

Breathe in the magic, let it flow,
Through whispered winds that come and go.
Each moment, a treasure to hold,
In shimmering stories, bright and bold.

Dance of the Infinite

In every step, the cosmos twirls,
Galaxies spin, as stardust whirls.
A dance that knows no start or end,
With every heartbeat, we transcend.

Looping time in a spiral embrace,
Each movement leaves a glowing trace.
Boundless skies draw us near,
In infinite patterns, crystal clear.

Together, we leap beyond the void,
Where dreams are born, and fears destroyed.
In this dance, forever free,
We find our place, just you and me.

Awash in Color

In the dawn's soft embrace, hues collide,
Whispers of warmth where shadows reside.
Petals unfurl, a delicate sigh,
Nature's canvas beneath the sky.

Fingers of sunlight paint every leaf,
Crafting a scene that brings sweet relief.
Rivers of crimson and gold cascade,
A symphony bright that will never fade.

Clouds drift like dreams, colored in grace,
Each moment a treasure, time's gentle trace.
Brushstrokes of joy in the air align,
Awash in color, everything divine.

As day turns to night, stars spark and gleam,
Every shadow holds a secret dream.
In twilight's embrace, emotions flow,
Awash in color, hearts gently glow.

Unfurling the Spirit

With each breath, a new story begins,
Layers of doubt fall, the journey spins.
Awakening softly, the soul takes flight,
Unfurling the spirit, embracing the light.

In the whispers of wind, truth finds a way,
Nurtured by moonlight, dreams drift and sway.
Every heartbeat a rhythm, strong and bold,
Carving out paths where wonders unfold.

Through valleys of silence, courage will rise,
Dance with the shadows, reach for the skies.
Unraveling tales in the heart's gentle beat,
Unfurling the spirit, making us complete.

In moments of stillness, wisdom ignites,
Guiding our souls on long, starry nights.
Awake to the magic, the love that's near,
Unfurling the spirit, shedding all fear.

Tapestry of Tiny Triumphs

Each day a stitch in the fabric of time,
Woven with purpose, each moment a rhyme.
Tiny triumphs, like stars, they gleam,
Threads of resilience in the grander scheme.

From whispers of kindness to laughter shared,
Each step forward shows we truly cared.
In the quiet moments, stories unfold,
A tapestry rich with silver and gold.

With every challenge and every small win,
A pattern emerges, where hope can begin.
Colors of courage blend, intertwine,
Tapestry of tiny triumphs, divine.

So celebrate each stitch, each thread's embrace,
For they weave together the heart of our space.
In life's gentle dance, take time to behold,
A tapestry woven, a journey retold.

Breezes of Contentedness

In the still of the morning, a breath of calm,
Nature's soft whispers, a soothing balm.
Breezes of contentedness fill the air,
Lifting spirits lightly, free from despair.

The rustle of leaves plays a gentle tune,
Comforting hearts beneath the bright moon.
Swaying of branches speaks of sweet ease,
Reminding us softly of life's little pleas.

In fields bathed in sunlight, dreams take their flight,
Dancing with joy in the warm, golden light.
Breezes of laughter, a symphony grand,
Carrying wishes from this tranquil land.

So breathe in the moment, let worries unfurl,
In the breezes of contentedness, let life swirl.
For peace is a treasure, held close and near,
In nature's embrace, everything's clear.

Echoes of Laughter

In the warm glow of twilight,
Laughter dances on the breeze,
Chasing shadows into the night,
Whispers of joy in the trees.

Children's giggles fill the air,
Moments lost, yet never fade,
Each echo a silent prayer,
In memories, love is conveyed.

Under the stars, secrets shared,
Every heartbeat, a song entwined,
In each smile, tenderly bared,
Echoes of happiness aligned.

As the moonlight softly gleams,
Laughter lingers, ever bright,
In the fabric of our dreams,
We weave together pure delight.

Mosaic of Memories

Pieces of time, a vivid scene,
Fragments of laughter and pain,
Each tile reflects who we've been,
In the sun, in the rain.

Colors blend in a design,
Tales of love and long goodbyes,
Within the chaos, we find rhyme,
In every glance, a shared surprise.

Stories linger in the air,
Whispers of joy, shadows of woe,
In our hearts, we gently care,
A mosaic that continues to grow.

While the years may fadeaway,
And moments slip through our hands,
In this tapestry, we will stay,
Bound by the life that we planned.

Infusion of Delight

A sip of sunshine on the tongue,
Sweetness bursts, a joyful sound,
In every moment, laughter sprung,
In the chaos, bliss is found.

The warmth of friendship, a soft glow,
Comfort wrapped like a new shawl,
In every heart, a gentle flow,
An infusion that embraces all.

Beneath the storm, we find our peace,
Tiny joys, they come alive,
In every smile, sweet release,
For here, our spirits truly thrive.

With every taste, the world expands,
Every breath a chance to sing,
In the dance of life, hand in hands,
We savor the love that we bring.

Harmony in the Everyday

Morning light spills gentle rays,
Hues of gold on quiet streets,
In the hustle, peace always stays,
In every heartbeat, rhythm repeats.

Simple moments, threads of grace,
Tying us to the here and now,
In the chaos, we find our place,
Embracing life's humble vow.

As the clock ticks, time goes slow,
In laughter shared, burdens lift,
In every smile, seeds we sow,
In the mundane, a precious gift.

With open hearts, we find the way,
Amidst the clatter, love will stay,
In unity, we softly sway,
Creating harmony day by day.

Moments of Pure Delight

The sun dips low in a painted sky,
Children's laughter echoes nearby.
Footsteps dance on the soft green grass,
Time stands still, wishing it would last.

A sweet breeze whispers through the trees,
Lifting the joy, it carries with ease.
Colors bloom in a vibrant array,
Each fleeting moment, a bright bouquet.

In a cozy corner with friends so dear,
Every shared story has laughter near.
Cups raised high, a toast to all,
In these moments, we truly stand tall.

As day gently shifts into night,
Stars appear, a spark in the light.
With hearts full, we gather around,
In moments of pure delight, love is found.

Awakening to Wonder

Morning breaks with a gentle hue,
Soft whispers of dawn greet the view.
A world refreshed, so full of grace,
Inviting us all to embrace.

Tiny miracles in each bloom,
Nature sings, dispelling the gloom.
The chirping birds, a symphony new,
Awakening hearts to the wonder so true.

As glistening dewdrops catch the light,
Each moment unfolds, pure and bright.
Inhaling peace, we stand and behold,
Life's simple magic is pure gold.

With every step, we find surprises,
In the small things, life truly rises.
Awakening senses to all around,
In every heartbeat, love is found.

Celebration of the Present

In every heartbeat, life's melody plays,
A canvas bright in sunlit rays.
With friends by our side, we lift a cheer,
Embracing each moment, holding it near.

The clinking of glasses, a toast to now,
Living fiercely, we take our vow.
Let laughter spill like a river wide,
In this celebration, we take pride.

As dreams unfold in the here and now,
We dance in rhythm, we're lost in the how.
With open hearts, we soak in the bliss,
The present is a treasure, none can dismiss.

Beneath the stars, we gather as one,
Grateful for all that we've quietly won.
In the tapestry of laughter and light,
We celebrate life, pure and bright.

Harmony in Simplicity

A gentle breeze rustles the leaves,
Whispers of peace in nature's eaves.
With barefoot walks on a path so clear,
Harmony blooms as the heart draws near.

The laughter of children playing outside,
Simple joys that we cannot hide.
A soft smile shared as we pause to see,
In moments of stillness, we are truly free.

With hands entwined, we sit by the stream,
Lost in a moment, like a sweet dream.
The world slows down, and we simply breathe,
In harmony's arms, we quietly weave.

As the sun dips low, painting the sky,
We feel the magic of time passing by.
In life's simplest gifts, we find our way,
In harmony's echo, we long to stay.

Untamed Bliss

In fields where wildflowers sway,
A dance of colors bright and free.
The whispers of the gentle breeze,
Call out to hearts in harmony.

Beneath the vast and open skies,
Where laughter rings like chimes at play.
Each moment sings a sweet surprise,
Embraced by love in wild array.

The sun dips low, a golden hue,
As twilight paints the world anew.
In every heartbeat lies a chance,
To lose ourselves in nature's dance.

With open arms, we wander free,
In untamed bliss we find our way.
The earth, our canvas, wild and grand,
In every step, a magic planned.

Light-dusted Paths

Along the lanes where shadows lie,
Soft beams of sun do gently fall.
Each step encounters whispers low,
A world awakened, nature's call.

The trees, like guardians, stand tall,
Their branches weave a golden thread.
In twinkling lights, the paths reveal,
A journey where our hearts are led.

With every breath, the air feels pure,
A melody of life unfolds.
The mysteries of time endure,
In stories that the earth still holds.

We wander through this sacred space,
Where light and shadow find their dance.
Each moment here, a shared embrace,
On light-dusted paths, we take a chance.

Cherished Breaths

In stillness where the heartbeats blend,
We find the warmth of memories shared.
Each cherished breath, a quiet bond,
In moments where our souls have bared.

Through laughter's echo and soft sighs,
In whispered dreams and fleeting glances,
We hold the fleeting joys and cries,
And treasure all the sweet advances.

The world may rush with frantic pace,
Yet in our hearts, time softly slows.
With every breath, we find our place,
In love that through the ages flows.

With gratitude, we greet the day,
For every breath that brings us near.
In sacred spaces, come what may,
We find the light, we hold it dear.

Colors of Today

A canvas bright, the dawn awakes,
In hues of gold and bursts of red.
Each moment speaks, a vibrant stroke,
In every smile, where joys are bred.

The laughter shared, a brilliant shade,
As friends unite in sunlit plays.
With every heart, a new hue made,
In colors bold that change our ways.

Through storms and sun, we paint our tales,
In brushstrokes fierce, and soft caress.
In every heartbeat, life prevails,
A tapestry of joy and stress.

So here we stand, in bright display,
Embracing all the shades of life.
Together, we create the day,
In colors rich, amidst the strife.

Beneath the Surface

In the depths where shadows play,
Secrets whisper night and day.
Colors dance in muted shades,
Life emerges, never fades.

Gentle ripples touch the shore,
Echoes of the ocean's roar.
Silent worlds beneath our feet,
Beauty wrapped in calm retreat.

Creatures glide in fluid grace,
Every corner, a hidden place.
Mysteries in turquoise gleam,
Beneath the surface, we dream.

What lies deep is yet unknown,
A universe all its own.
In the stillness, we discover,
Wonders that we long to uncover.

Vibrations of Fulfillment

In the heart where dreams reside,
Whispers of hope do not hide.
Each moment sings a sweet refrain,
Echoes of joy in every vein.

Stars align in cosmic dance,
Life unfolds in every chance.
The pulse of earth, the rhythm true,
In harmony, we find our cue.

Grains of sand, the timeless flow,
Waves of love, they come and go.
In the embrace of night and day,
Fulfillment blooms, lighting the way.

Know the power of your voice,
In the silence, we rejoice.
Let each vibration guide your path,
Feel the spark, embrace the wrath.

Nature's Soft Caress

Gentle breeze through leaves does glide,
Nature's warmth, our hearts confide.
In the stillness, whispers rise,
Soft caress 'neath open skies.

Petals fall like dreams in flight,
Sunset paints the approaching night.
Mountains cradle clouds so high,
Nature's lullaby, a sigh.

Rivers dance on stones so clear,
Each ripple holds a memory dear.
In the forest, shadows creep,
All the secrets that they keep.

Find your peace in every breath,
In the cycle, life and death.
Nature's touch, a sacred space,
In stillness, find your grace.

Hollow Echoes of Elysium

Silence falls where laughter used to be,
Hollow echoes whisper endlessly.
In this void, the shadows talk,
Remnants of the sacred walk.

Ghostly trails of dreams once spun,
Faded hopes beneath the sun.
In the twilight, memories fade,
Promises that we once made.

Stars above in silent watch,
Time slips by, no hearts to clutch.
Elysium lost in distant haze,
Longing for those golden days.

Yet in shadows, lessons lie,
From the ashes, we'll still fly.
In the echoes, truth does gleam,
Hollow whispers, yet we dream.

Mirth in the Mundane

In every drop of morning dew,
A sparkle waits, fresh and new.
The simple joys, they call to me,
In life's routine, I find the key.

A child's laughter fills the air,
A reminder that we all care.
A moment shared, a smile's glow,
In tiny things, our hearts can grow.

The rhythm of the ticking clock,
Each second sings, a gentle rock.
Through busy streets, I wander free,
In every face, a story's plea.

The everyday, a canvas wide,
With colors bold and hearts as guides.
Embrace the small, the calm, the plain,
For in the mundane, joy remains.

Embracing Sunset's Warmth

The day retreats, a golden hue,
Painting the sky in shades so true.
A gentle breeze begins to play,
As night whispers the close of day.

The sun dips low, in fiery glow,
Arranging all its colors so.
With every shade a story's told,
In warmth of light, our hearts unfold.

Birds return to nests up high,
Underneath the canvas sky.
The world calms down, a hush descends,
With every sunset, peace extends.

Embrace the twilight's gentle breath,
As day surrenders, welcoming rest.
In quiet moments, find your worth,
For in the dusk, there's magic's birth.

Whispers of Existence

In silence, secrets soft arise,
The rustle of leaves, nature's sighs.
The world speaks low in shades of green,
In every heartbeat, life is seen.

A quiet stream flows without haste,
Carving the rocks, life's gentle pace.
Each ripple tells a tale of old,
In whispers of existence, bold.

The night's embrace, a twinkling sky,
Stars wink softly, a lullaby.
Each pinprick light, a dreamer's wish,
In the cosmos' vast, we find our bliss.

Listen closely, to the winds that speak,
In every shadow, the stories peek.
Whispers linger, in hearts that yearn,
In the dance of life, we take our turn.

Dancing with Shadows

At twilight's hour, they come alive,
Shadows sway, as dreams revive.
In moonlit grace, they twist and twirl,
Inviting all to join their whirl.

The darkened corners hold their tales,
Of whispered fears and ancient trails.
With every step, a story spins,
In shadow's dance, the night begins.

Flickering lights, a playful guide,
In the stillness, we confide.
With each pirouette, a secret shared,
In the shadows, we are spared.

Embrace the dusk, let worries fade,
In twilight's arms, we're unafraid.
For in this dance, we find our way,
With shadows close, we learn to sway.

Whirlwinds of Wonder

In the dance of the leaves, they swirl,
Hints of secrets in every twirl.
Voices whisper in the gentle breeze,
Nature sings as the heart finds ease.

Clouds drift softly across the sky,
Chasing shadows where dreams lie.
Each moment a treasure, a gift so rare,
In the embrace of the world, we share.

Mountains echo the call of the wild,
Each path leads where silence smiled.
With every heartbeat, the earth spins round,
In whirlwinds of wonder, joy is found.

Sparkling stars in the night so clear,
Remind us of all we hold dear.
Under the moon, we dance and play,
In the magic of now, we find our way.

Savoring the Now

Each sunrise glimmers with golden light,
Nature wakes softly from the night.
Morning dew clings to blades of grass,
In the moment, let the worries pass.

Conversations filled with laughter's sound,
In the simple joy, true love is found.
With every breath, the beauty grows,
Savoring the now, the heart openly knows.

Time dances lightly, no rush, no chase,
In this fleeting moment, we find our place.
Grains of sand slip through our hands,
Learning the magic in life's simple plans.

Let us pause, take a mindful breath,
Relishing life, embracing its depth.
In the now, our spirits align,
Every fleeting second, a treasure divine.

Celebrating the Unseen

In whispers of wind, the stories bloom,
In shadows where light makes room.
Hidden paths that call us near,
Celebrating the magic we hold dear.

The heart beats softly, a gentle thrum,
In the silence, the wonders come.
Every glance holds a world apart,
In unseen realms, we find the heart.

Beneath the surface, life unfolds,
In tales of the brave, the quiet and bold.
Invisible threads weave us as one,
In the unseen, a journey begun.

With open eyes, we start to see,
The beauty that lies in you and me.
Together we dance, in joyful air,
Celebrating the unseen, with love to share.

Joyful Journeys

Each step we take on this winding road,
Leads to wonders waiting to be bestowed.
In laughter, in tears, we find our way,
Joyful journeys paint the world in play.

Mountains rise high, valleys dip low,
With every passage, our hearts will grow.
Friendships blossom under the sun,
In the dance of life, we're all but one.

Across the oceans, where dreams take flight,
Adventure calls in the soft twilight.
With every heartbeat, the world unfolds,
In joyful journeys, the story is told.

Embrace the moments, let spirits soar,
In the celebration, we seek for more.
Together we wander, forever to roam,
Finding our way, making the world home.

Gratitude in Each Heartbeat

In quiet moments, I find grace,
Each heartbeat whispers, a warm embrace.
Thankful for the dawn's gentle light,
For love that stirs in the still of night.

In laughter shared and smiles so bright,
In simple joys that feel just right.
The beauty in the smallest things,
In every gift that each day brings.

With every sigh, a prayer takes flight,
Gratitude glows, a radiant sight.
I cherish each breath, each serene start,
This deep-seated joy within my heart.

Life's hurried pace may fade away,
Yet gratitude here will ever stay.
In memories etched and dreams that soar,
I find my peace, forevermore.

Transcending the Mundane

In the clock's tick, magic hides,
Within the routine, wonder abides.
A mundane walk, a step divine,
Each moment shines when we align.

The rustling leaves, a soft caress,
Transforming the drab into finesse.
Through simple acts, we cultivate,
A sacred space where dreams await.

Breath by breath, out of the gray,
We weave the magic into our day.
In every glance, a chance to see,
The beauty in life's tapestry.

In the ordinary, we will find,
The extraordinary intertwined.
So lift your gaze, let spirits sing,
The mundane holds its hidden wing.

Nurtured by Nature

Amidst the trees, my heart takes flight,
In each green leaf, a world of light.
Rivers whisper secrets, deep and true,
Nature's embrace, a love anew.

In mountains high, my spirit roams,
The quiet calls, a place called home.
With every sunset, colors blend,
A canvas where the heavens send.

The flowers dance in gentle breeze,
In nature's song, I find my peace.
With every dawn, the skies unfold,
Stories of warmth and tales of old.

Nurtured by earth, by sky, by sea,
In nature's arms, I long to be.
A symphony of life, profound,
In every heartbeat, nature's sound.

Heartbeats and Daydreams

In quiet corners of my mind,
Daydreams swirl, a path to find.
With every heartbeat, dreams take flight,
On wings of hope, in soft twilight.

Imagined worlds where lovers meet,
And starlit skies feel warm and sweet.
In whispered thoughts, I roam afar,
Chasing wishes, each shining star.

Time slows down in this sacred space,
Heartbeats echo in gentle grace.
Reality drifts, like clouds that sway,
In daydreams' arms, I'm free to play.

With every sigh, the heart will weave,
Tales of longing that we believe.
In this dance of dreams, I seek,
The solace found in moments meek.

Laughter in the Quiet

In the stillness, laughter blooms,
Soft echoes fill the empty rooms.
A gentle breeze stirs up the light,
Whispers dance through day and night.

Joy teeters on the edge of calm,
Filling hearts, a quiet balm.
In shared glances, we find our song,
A melody where we belong.

Through quiet hours, the spark ignites,
Brightening shadows as it bites.
In every chuckle, warmth unfolds,
Creating stories yet untold.

Laughter lingers, soft and sweet,
A tapestry of hearts that meet.
In the silence, joy's refrain,
We find solace in the same.

Infinite Possibilities

In the dawn of day, I stand awake,
Wondering what paths my soul may take.
Each choice like stars, shining bright,
Guiding me through the endless night.

With every breath, a chance to see,
All the worlds that could ever be.
Horizons whisper, dreams expire,
Leaving trails woven with desire.

A paper boat on the flowing stream,
Drifting onward, chasing dreams.
With every turn, the journey swells,
Echoing secrets in whispered spells.

Infinite stories yet untold,
Await beyond the morning gold.
With open arms, the universe calls,
To dance with grace before it falls.

Savoring Simple Moments

A cup of tea in the morning glow,
Silent seconds, let them slow.
Raindrops tap on the windowpane,
Carving paths in sweet refrain.

The laughter shared in twilight's haze,
Softly wrapped in golden rays.
Nature's whispers, gentle, clear,
Moments cherished, held so dear.

In the rustle of leaves overhead,
Life's quiet miracles are spread.
Each breath a treasure, slowly found,
In simple joys, our hearts abound.

The warmth of hands in evening's light,
Comforting shadows, soft and bright.
Savoring time, a gentle art,
Painting love within the heart.

Radiant Threads of Being

In the fabric of life, threads entwine,
Colorful stories form the divine.
Each moment stitched with intention clear,
Radiates warmth, drawing us near.

Through trials borne, the fibers grow,
Embracing strength in ebb and flow.
In twilight's glow, we weave our tale,
A tapestry rich, where dreams prevail.

Gratitude glimmers in every seam,
Binding our hearts, igniting the dream.
In laughter and tears, brilliance appears,
A radiant journey through joy and fears.

As new threads enter, the story expands,
Crafted with love by gentle hands.
Together we soar, always believing,
In the beauty of radiant weaving.

Spontaneous Joyrides

Open road beneath bright skies,
Adventure calls as laughter flies.
Windows down, we feel the breeze,
Moments like these are meant to seize.

With each turn, thrill on our face,
Chasing dreams at a wild pace.
Fueling joy with every mile,
Life's a journey, let's embrace the style.

Music plays, hearts beat as one,
Underneath the glowing sun.
Unplanned stops, the world to see,
Spontaneous joy, wild and free.

Through winding paths and open space,
These joyrides bring a warm embrace.
Side by side, our spirits soar,
In each moment, we crave more.

A Poem for Every Sunrise

Each dawn brings a brand new gift,
Golden rays, our spirits lift.
Colors dance across the sky,
A painted canvas, oh so high.

Morning whispers through the trees,
Softly swaying with the breeze.
Promises of what's to come,
With every beam, the heart can hum.

Nature calls with gentle grace,
Every sunrise finds its place.
Awakening dreams, a chance to rise,
With gratitude in our eyes.

Embrace the day, let worries fade,
In every hue, life's serenade.
For every sunrise, a chance to dream,
An endless flow, a magic stream.

Radiance of Routine

In the rhythm of everyday,
We find comfort in the play.
Morning coffee, gentle sighs,
A simple joy that never dies.

A quiet walk, familiar ground,
In small moments, peace is found.
Schedule's dance, a steady beat,
In routine's warmth, our hearts meet.

The clock ticks soft, yet loud enough,
In monotony, life isn't tough.
Each task holds a secret glow,
In daily life, love can grow.

Embrace the grace in each small act,
In routine's fold, we find our pact.
With open hearts, we celebrate,
In radiance, we cultivate.

Leaves of Laughter

In the breeze, they dance and sway,
Leaves of laughter, come what may.
Joyful sounds in the crisp air,
Echoing moments, beyond compare.

Beneath the trees, we share delight,
Playful whispers, hearts take flight.
Autumn's glow, a joyful cheer,
Laughter wraps us, warm and near.

Colors change, yet laughter stays,
In every season, love conveys.
Crunch of leaves beneath our feet,
A melody that feels so sweet.

Gather 'round, let stories flow,
Through laughter's leaves, our spirits grow.
In every chuckle, joy ignites,
Celebrating life's simple delights.

Radiant Moments Unfold

In the dawn's warm embrace, we rise,
Whispers of hope dance in the skies.
Each heartbeat a treasure, a story to tell,
Moments like these, in our hearts they dwell.

Joy blooms like flowers, vibrant and bright,
Chasing away shadows, igniting the light.
With laughter that sparkles, we share in the bliss,
Radiant moments, too precious to miss.

Time flows like rivers, serene in its grace,
Sharing our dreams, we find our place.
In this fleeting world, we gather and hold,
Memories treasured, as radiant as gold.

Together we wander through life's gentle stream,
Finding our magic, fulfilling the dream.
In every encounter, love softly unfolds,
Creating a tapestry, woven with gold.

A Symphony of Breaths

In the quiet twilight, whispers take flight,
A symphony grows, rich and bright.
Breaths intertwine like the notes of a song,
Together we dance, where we all belong.

Each heartbeat a rhythm, each sigh a refrain,
Moments of stillness amidst the mundane.
In the fabric of life, we weave and we spin,
Creating a melody, a harmony within.

With nature as chorus, the stars in the night,
Guiding our journey, illuminating sight.
In silence and sound, we find our true voice,
In this grand symphony, we all rejoice.

Let the music of moments echo and soar,
A testament of love, to cherish and adore.
In every breath taken, a story bestowed,
A symphony alive, where our spirits flowed.

Luminous Days

Under the sun's gentle rays, we bask,
Life's little wonders, no need to ask.
With every sunrise, a chance to ignite,
Luminous days, bathed in pure light.

The laughter of children plays in the breeze,
Carrying joy like leaves from the trees.
In simple moments, we find our way,
As time gently dances through luminous days.

With friends gathered close, hearts open wide,
We share stories told with love as our guide.
Echoes of memories in laughter and cheer,
Creating a warmth that always draws near.

In the twilight's glow, we reflect and sigh,
Wishing these luminous days never say goodbye.
Let us cherish the light, the warmth from above,
In every heartbeat, we celebrate love.

Inherent Bliss

In the quiet corners of our mind's eye,
Lies a gentle stillness, a soothing sigh.
Inherent bliss wrapped in moments so sweet,
Found in simple pleasures, our hearts meet.

Beneath the vast skies, we breathe and create,
A canvas of dreams where we are innate.
In every sunrise, a promise shines through,
Guiding our souls with a love that is true.

With gratitude whispered on each passing breeze,
Worlds of our making, where life's heart can freeze.
In laughter and kindness, we find our way,
Inherent bliss lives in each joyful play.

So let us drink deeply from this well of grace,
Embracing the journey, each radiant space.
Wherever we wander, our spirits align,
Inherent bliss blooms, forever divine.

Nature's Gentle Lullaby

The whispering winds softly sway,
Carrying dreams where the shadows play.
Moonlit rivers reflect the night,
Crickets sing in soft delight.

Beneath the stars, the world is still,
Nature's heart, a calm to fill.
Leaves rustle with a soothing sound,
In this peace, our souls are bound.

A gentle breeze, a sweet refrain,
Echoes softly, easing pain.
Nature's voice, a warm embrace,
Guides us to a tranquil place.

So close your eyes and drift away,
Let nature's lullaby display.
In every heartbeat, in every sigh,
Life unfolds beneath the sky.

Emblems of Euphoria

Joy blooms brightly like a rose,
In every smile, our spirit grows.
Laughter dances, light as air,
Moments treasured, sweet and rare.

Sunlight spills on golden fields,
Nature's bounty, joy it yields.
Every heartbeat, a vibrant chord,
In every thread, our hopes restored.

With friends beside, the world feels bright,
In shared memories, pure delight.
Emblems of love, woven tight,
Together shining, hearts in flight.

Every sunset brings a glow,
In life's canvas, colors flow.
Embrace each day, let spirits soar,
For in this joy, we seek for more.

Treasures of the Present

Time slips by like grains of sand,
In each moment, life is planned.
Cherish now, let worries cease,
In this now, find your peace.

Glimmers of laughter, sparks of joy,
In simple things, find your ploy.
A friend's embrace, a sunset's glow,
These tiny treasures help us grow.

Each heartbeat echoes, time's embrace,
In fleeting moments, find your place.
Breathe in deep, let worries fade,
In the now, true treasures laid.

So hold on tight to this sweet bliss,
In every hug or simple kiss.
Life's joys whisper, softly call,
Treasures of the present, cherish all.

Moments That Sing

In twilight's glow, the crickets play,
A serenade for the end of day.
Stars awaken, shining bright,
Moments that sing in the deep of night.

Laughter bubbles like a stream,
In every glance, a whispered dream.
Time stands still, as we embrace,
These fleeting moments, love's sweet grace.

Echoes of joy in every smile,
Let's celebrate, if just for a while.
Each heartbeat dances, a gentle throng,
In life's melody, where we belong.

So gather close, let stories flow,
In shared moments, let love grow.
For life's a song, meant to be sung,
In memory's heart, forever young.

Radiance of Existence

In the dawn's gentle light, we rise,
Each moment a gift, a sweet surprise.
Stars fade softly, dreams take flight,
In this vast world, we find our might.

Through shadows cast by time and fate,
We seek the paths where love awaits.
With open hearts, we face the day,
In every heartbeat, joy will stay.

Nature's whispers call us near,
In every sound, a song to hear.
Beneath the sky, we dance and play,
Radiant souls, come what may.

Embrace the now, let worries cease,
In the stillness, find your peace.
Life's vibrant brush paints with grace,
In every corner, beauty's face.

Embracing Every Breath

With every breath, we claim our space,
In the rhythm of life, we find our pace.
A gentle sigh, a laugh, a tear,
In this great tapestry, all is clear.

Moments linger, fleeting yet sweet,
In the chaos, we find our beat.
Hold on to joy, let go of pain,
In love's embrace, we break the chain.

Time flows like a river, so wide,
In each current, let hope reside.
Together we journey, hand in hand,
In the symphony, we take a stand.

Cherish the now, as it sweeps away,
In every heartbeat, find your way.
Embracing life, in all its worth,
A sacred dance, our shared rebirth.

Whispers of Contentment

In quiet corners, peace takes flight,
Whispers of contentment, soft and light.
Each moment savored, a gentle sigh,
In this humble space, we learn to fly.

Beneath the stars, dreams softly weave,
In the warmth of night, our hearts believe.
Silent echoes of love's embrace,
In tranquil hours, we find our place.

The beauty in stillness, a soothing balm,
In nature's arms, we feel the calm.
With every breath, a story spun,
In the dance of life, we are one.

Gratitude flows like a gentle stream,
In the fabric of existence, we dream.
Whispers of joy, forever to stay,
In the heart's chamber, lighting the way.

Dancing in the Now

Step by step, the world unfolds,
In the present moment, stories told.
With laughter echoing, spirits soar,
Dancing through life, forevermore.

In every heartbeat, in every glance,
We find the courage, we take the chance.
With open arms, we greet the day,
In vibrant colors, we choose to play.

The rhythm of now, a sacred beat,
In the magic of life, we find our feet.
Together we twirl, through joy and strife,
Dancing the tapestry, a precious life.

So let go of worries, let your heart sing,
In the flow of existence, feel the spring.
Dancing in the now, we beautifully flow,
In this dance of life, we truly glow.

Rhapsody of the Ordinary

In the hum of daily life, we sing,
A song of simple joys and what they bring.
The scent of rain on thirsty ground,
In ordinary moments, beauty is found.

A cup of tea, the morning light,
A friend's warm smile that feels so right.
These fleeting hours weave stories true,
In the rhapsody of all we do.

A gentle breeze, nature's embrace,
In quiet corners, we find our place.
The rustle of leaves, a lover's tune,
In ordinary days, beneath the moon.

So let us dance in this gentle glow,
Embracing all, as we come and go.
For in this life, both rich and bland,
A symphony of moments, hand in hand.

Glimmers of Elation

A sparkle caught in a child's eye,
Laughter bubbles, a sweet goodbye.
The sun dips low, painting the sky,
In fleeting moments, we learn to fly.

Each dewdrop holds the dawn's sweet kiss,
A whisper of joy, a perfect bliss.
We chase the light where shadows fade,
In glimmers of elation, life's serenade.

The flutter of wings, the song of a breeze,
A heart that dances among the trees.
Collecting fragments of time's embrace,
In laughter and love, we find our place.

So let us grasp these flickering dreams,
A tapestry woven with sunlit beams.
In every heartbeat, joy's refrain,
In glimmers of elation, no room for pain.

Footprints in the Sand

Waves brush softly on a golden shore,
Each footprint whispers tales of yore.
Moments linger in the salty breeze,
In patterns left by wandering feet.

The sun sets slow, painting the sea,
Each step reflects who we came to be.
The tide may wash our tracks away,
But memories linger, come what may.

Shells glisten bright under fading light,
Each a reminder, a precious sight.
Time moves on, but we leave our trace,
In footprints etched, we find our place.

So walk the shore, let your spirit roam,
In grains of sand, we craft our home.
Though the waves may steal what we've bestowed,
Our journeys remain, wherever we go.

Chasing Fireflies

In twilight's hush, we dance and play,
With fireflies lighting our secret way.
Each flicker sparkles, a fleeting star,
In summer's embrace, we wander far.

Laughter rings out, a joyful sound,
As a thousand lights twirl round and round.
We reach for dreams, in the warm night air,
Chasing shadows, without a care.

The night sky wraps us in velvet blue,
Each tiny glow, a wish anew.
In hearts of children, wonder ignites,
As we chase fireflies into the nights.

So hold the magic as long as we can,
In the dance of youth, we find our plan.
With every flicker, our spirits rise,
In chasing fireflies, we learn to fly.

Serenade of the Ordinary

In the morning light, a breeze flows,
Whispers of life in simple prose.
Every bird sings, an ordinary tune,
As shadows dance beneath the moon.

Children play on streets of dust,
In laughter and joy, we find our trust.
A cup of tea, warm in hand,
Moments cherished, as life is planned.

Old trees sway with tales untold,
Hearts grow warm as friendships unfold.
In the mundane, beauty you'll find,
A serenade, gentle and kind.

Life's melody, in every beat,
In ordinary moments, we feel complete.
Each day a gift, wrapped in grace,
In the simplest things, we find our place.

Euphoria in Stillness

In quiet corners, peace descends,
The heart unwinds, its rhythm mends.
Through stillness vast, the mind takes flight,
In whispers soft, we greet the night.

Stars above, a canvas wide,
In silence deep, our souls confide.
Each breath a wave, a tranquil sea,
In the hush of dusk, we find the key.

Nature holds a timeless space,
Where calmness glows, a warm embrace.
In solitude, the world feels right,
Euphoria blooms in the soft twilight.

With every moment of purest rest,
We find our center, our hearts are blessed.
In stillness found, our spirits grow,
Euphoria in the quiet flow.

Unfolding in Laughter

Joy erupts like flowers in spring,
With laughter's dance, our spirits sing.
Bright faces glow in vibrant cheer,
As echoes ring, the world feels near.

In playful banter, stories weave,
In every giggle, we learn to believe.
Moments shared, a tapestry bright,
Unfolding dreams in the soft twilight.

Life's simple joys, a treasure chest,
In laughter's glow, we feel the best.
With every joke, the day grows warm,
Unfolding joy, a happy charm.

Together we rise, like stars in the night,
In laughter's embrace, everything's right.
A symphony sweet, in pure delight,
Unfolding lives, in love's own light.

Essence of Serenity

Beneath the trees, a moment rests,
In nature's arms, the heart invests.
A gentle stream, a soothing sound,
In this embrace, peace can be found.

Clouds drift slowly across the sky,
In their soft journey, our worries fly.
Every leaf whispers a calming verse,
In stillness embraced, we disperse the curse.

As dawn breaks bright, the world awakens,
In serene beauty, our hearts are taken.
The essence of calm in every breath,
In quietude, we conquer death.

So let us pause, and simply be,
In the essence of serenity, we see.
Life unfolds in moments pure,
Embracing peace, we feel secure.

Reveling in Simple Pleasures

A warm sun kiss on my skin,
Laughter shared with close friends,
The scent of blooming flowers,
Moments that the heart ascends.

Sipping tea on a quiet day,
Chasing shadows, light as air,
The taste of joy in every sip,
Treasures found everywhere.

A soft breeze through the trees,
Children playing without a care,
The sound of waves against the shore,
Nature sings a sweet affair.

In each small moment, life unfolds,
Secrets whispered in the night,
Reveling in the simple things,
Bringing our souls pure delight.

The Art of Here and Now

In stillness, find the beating heart,
The world slows, a gentle pause,
Each breath a canvas to create,
A world revealed without a cause.

Embrace the warmth of morning light,
Feel the ground beneath your feet,
Existence blooms in present time,
Moments crafted, pure and sweet.

Listen close to the whispering winds,
Let worries drift, like clouds afloat,
This art of now, a silent dance,
Where every second is a note.

In the tapestry of being free,
Breathe in the magic, take a vow,
The present is a gift indeed,
Master the art of here and now.

Essence of the Everyday

Raindrops tapping on the glass,
A cup of coffee, warm embrace,
Familiar streets where stories dwell,
Life unfolds at easy pace.

A smile shared with strangers near,
The rustle of leaves in the breeze,
Colors splash in setting sun,
Each moment holds its own keys.

The rhythm of a life well-lived,
Echoes in the morning hum,
A child's laughter, pure delight,
In every heartbeat, we become.

Cherish the mundane, it shines bright,
In monotony's sweet refrains,
The essence of the everyday,
Lies in love, in joyful gains.

Serenade of the Soul

In twilight's glow, a secret song,
Whispers gentle, soft and low,
The serenade of twilight's grace,
Inviting hearts to ebb and flow.

A moonlit path, where dreams collide,
Stars are notes in night's sweet tune,
Every heartbeat echoes the bliss,
In the dance of shadow and moon.

With every breath, a story spun,
Of hopes and fears, of love untold,
The language of the heart, our muse,
A melody that never grows old.

So listen close, the night is young,
Let your spirit sway and soar,
In the serenade of the soul,
We find forever, evermore.

Milton Keynes UK
Ingram Content Group UK Ltd.
UKHW021939121124
451129UK00007B/147

9 789916 889862